"Those who are not shocked when they first come across quantum theory cannot possibly have understood it."

—NIELS BOHR
1885-1962

Published by Bushel & Peck Books, a family-run publishing house in Fresno, California, that believes in uplifting children with the highest standards of art, music, literature, and ideas. Find beautiful books for gifted young minds at www.bushelandpeckbooks.com.

Type set in Didot and Josefin Sans.

Illustrations are mixed-media digital collages with elements sourced from public domain galleries or licensed from Shutterstock.com. Additional visual credits: Marie Curie photograph (Science Museum Group/Wellcome); Albert Einstein photograph (United States Library of Congress); Atom comic book (National Archives); James Chadwick (Los Alamos National Laboratory: see https://www.lanl.gov/resources/web-policies/copyright-legal.php).

Bushel & Peck Books is dedicated to fighting illiteracy all over the world. For every book we sell, we donate one to a child in need—book for book. To nominate a school or organization to receive free books, please visit www.bushelandpeckbooks.com.

LCCN: 2021937891
ISBN: 9781638191001

First Edition

Printed in the United States

10 9 8 7 6 5 4 3 2 1

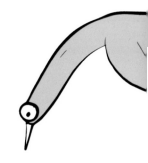

atom

*The Building Block
of the Universe*

DAVID MILES

**BUSHEL
& PECK
BOOKS**

Over there is an atom.

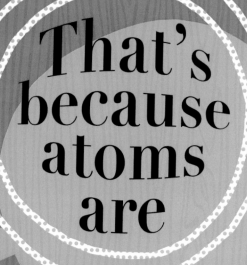

That's because atoms are

super,

super,

super,

super,

super

small.

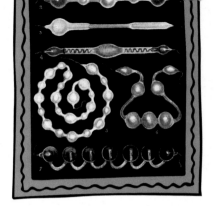

To see one, we'll have
to zoom in.

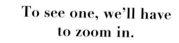

Go on . . . a
little more.

That's it. A little more.

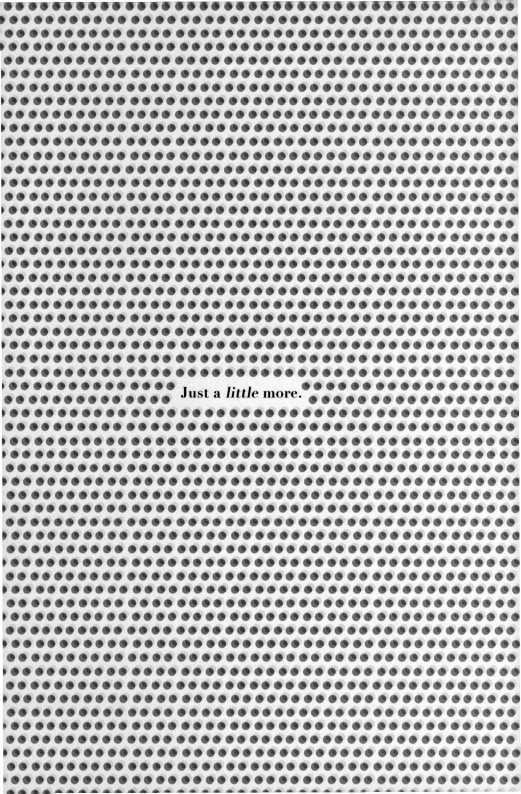

Just a *little* more.

Aaaaaaand . . .

THERE!

Do you see it now?

This is an atom. And it, my friend, is the building block of everything.

Atoms.

This painting?

Atoms.

This
tower?

You guessed it.

Ooh la . . .
waaaaah?

Everything in the entire

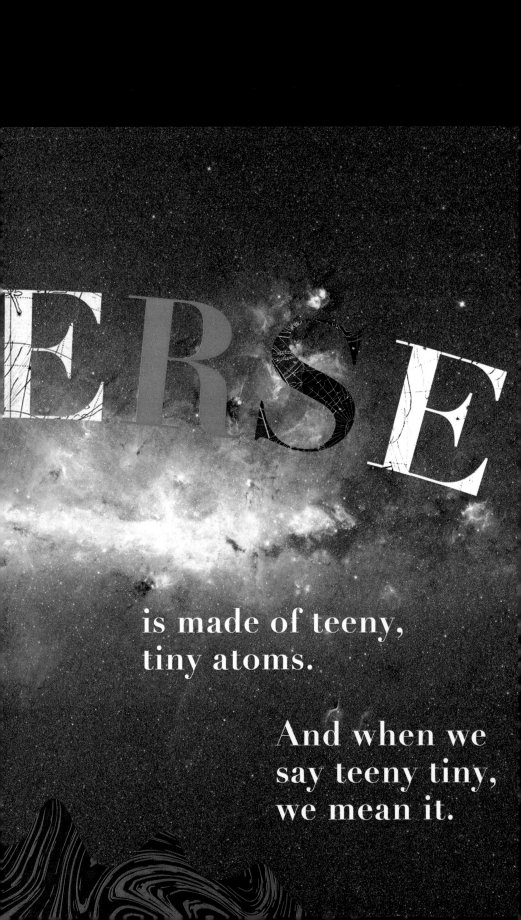

ERSE

is made of teeny,
tiny atoms.

And when we
say teeny tiny,
we mean it.

Look closely at this baseball.

Pretend you blew that baseball up until it was the size of the *whole* earth.

If its atoms grew at the same rate, they'd still be only the size of . . .

. . . a
blueberry.

All atoms have the same basic structure. At the center is the nucleus. Here, every atom has a certain number of particles called protons. Those have a positive charge.

Then, there is also usually* an equal number of neutrons — those have no charge.

Outside the nucleus are often** the same number of electrons, which have a negative charge.

*Hydrogen, for example, has only a single proton in the nucelus — no neutron!

**Atoms can sometimes end up with extra electrons (or sometimes *less* than the right amount, too). Those atoms are called *ions*.

ELECTRON

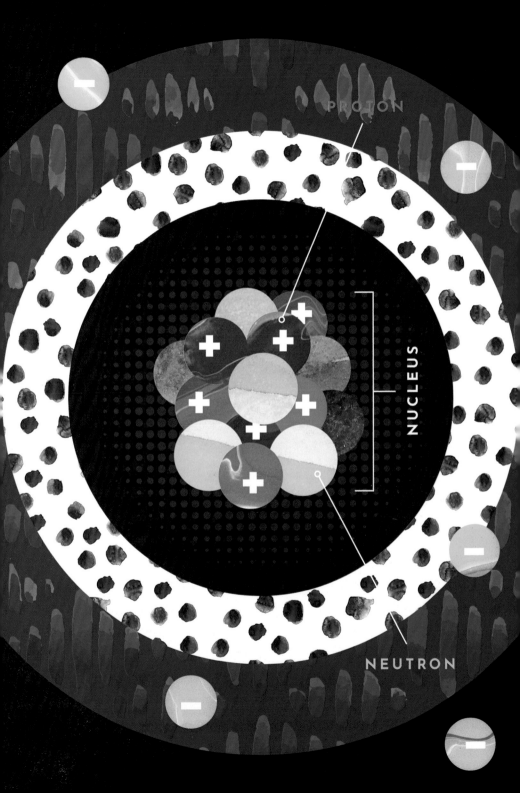

PROTON

NUCLEUS

NEUTRON

Niels Bohr proposed that electrons revolve around the nucleus in different orbits, like planets around the sun.

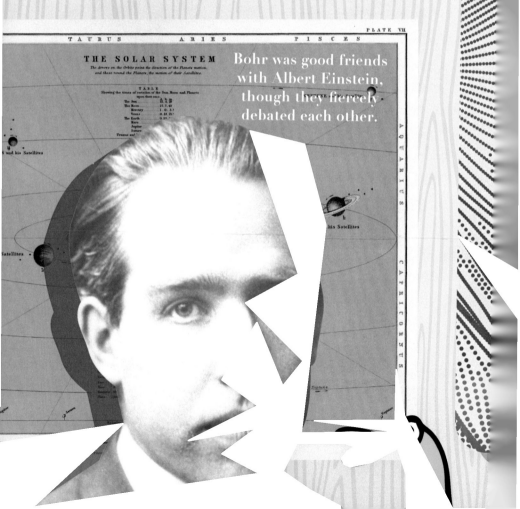

PLATE VII

TAURUS   ARIES   PISCES

THE SOLAR SYSTEM

The Arrows on the Orbits point the direction of the Planets motion, and those round the Planets, the motion of their Satellites.

TABLE

Showing the times of rotation of the Sun, Moon and Planets upon their axes.

Bohr was good friends with Albert Einstein, though they fiercely debated each other.

AQUARIUS

CAPRICORNUS

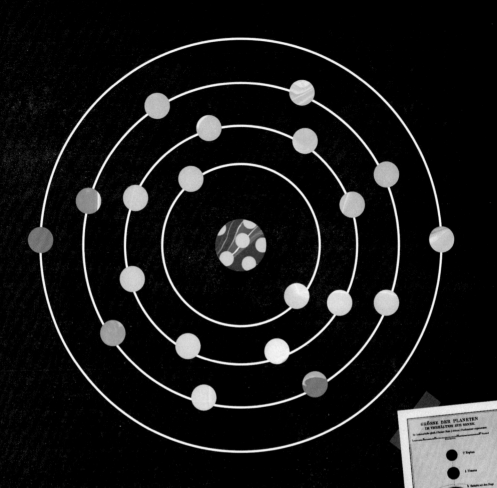

This is called the
planetary model.

However, because of work done by Erwin Schrödinger (and others), scientists now believe that electrons behave more like waves.

No, not those waves.

And no, Schrödinger probably never surfed, though he did love German poetry.

Think of the string on a guitar. When you pluck the string, it quivers back and forth with energy, even while the ends of the string stay stuck to the guitar.

Scientists believe that electrons act like the string, spread out as waves of vibrating energy.

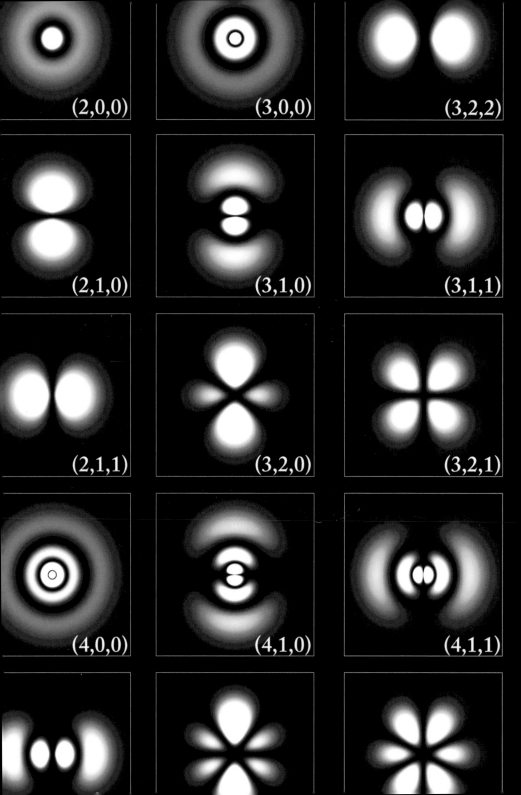

This is called the quantum mechanical model. And although scientists don't know *exactly* where the electrons are, they can use math to illustrate predictions.

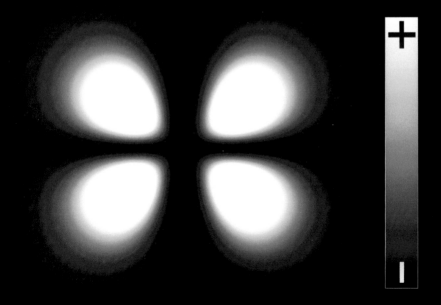

Where electrons are most likely to be.

+

I

Where electrons are least likely to be.

You might have noticed something: atoms come in many shapes and sizes.

WT 4.0026

SODIUM NET WT 22.990

LITHIUM NE

CUE FRO

ew
y
ARL

als

T WT 14.007

CHLORINE NET WT 35.45

OXYGEN N

The smallest atom has just one proton and one electron. Others have over a hundred!

A substance
made entirely
out of just one
type of atom
is called an
element.

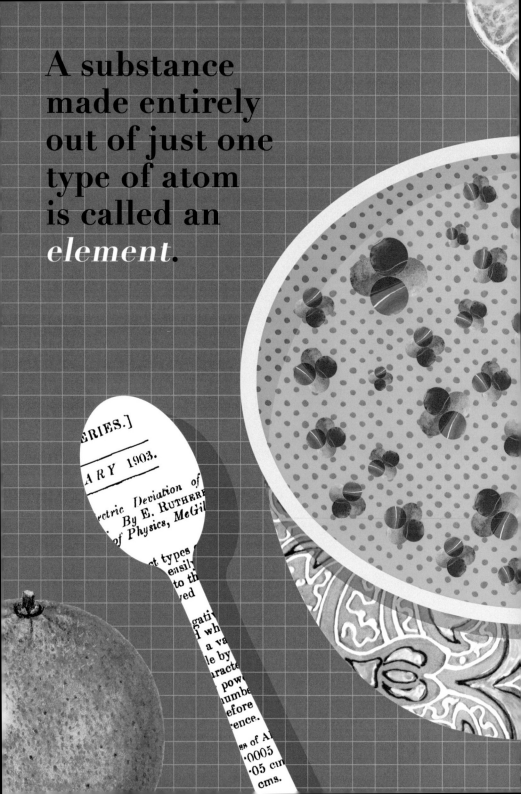

THEY FLOAT!

HELL-O'S

Let's take a look at a few different elements.

An atom of GOLD is made from seventy-nine protons, seventy-nine neutrons, and seventy-nine electrons.

Have you ever seen a lump of coal? That's mostly made of CARBON, which has six protons, six neutrons, and six electrons.

And the **HELIUM** inside a balloon is made from atoms with two protons, two neutrons, and two electrons.

Norman Lockyer is credited with helping to discover helium.

There are ninety-four elements that occur naturally in the world.

There are twenty-four more that scientists have created on their own.

24

How they do that is beyond the scope of this book, but it involves smashing atoms together at super-high speeds.

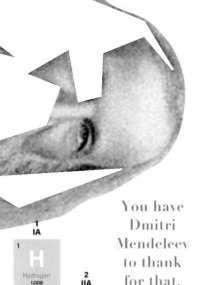

If that seems like a lot, don't worry! Over the years, scientists have built a simple chart to organize all the different elements they know of so far.

You have Dmitri Mendeleev to thank for that.

1 IA									
1 H Hydrogen 1.008	2 IIA								
3 Li Lithium 6.94	4 Be Beryllium 9.0121831								
11 Na Sodium 22.98976928	12 Mg Magnesium 24.305	3 IIIB	4 IVB	5 VB	6 VIB	7 VIIB	8 VIIIB	9 VIIIB	10 VIIIB
19 K Potassium 39.0983	20 Ca Calcium 40.078	21 Sc Scandium 44.955908	22 Ti Titanium 47.867	23 V Vanadium 50.9415	24 Cr Chromium 51.9961	25 Mn Manganese 54.938044	26 Fe Iron 55.845	27 Co Cobalt 58.933194	28 Ni Nickel 58.693
37 Rb Rubidium 85.4678	38 Sr Strontium 87.62	39 Y Yttrium 88.90584	40 Zr Zirconium 91.224	41 Nb Niobium 92.90637	42 Mo Molybdenum 95.95	43 Tc Technetium (98)	44 Ru Ruthenium 101.07	45 Rh Rhodium 102.90550	46 Pd Palladium 106.42
55 Cs Caesium 132.90545196	56 Ba Barium 137.327	57 - 71 Lanthanoids	72 Hf Hafnium 178.49	73 Ta Tantalum 180.94788	74 W Tungsten 183.84	75 Re Rhenium 186.207	76 Os Osmium 190.23	77 Ir Iridium 192.217	78 Pt Platinum 195.084
87 Fr Francium (223)	88 Ra Radium (226)	89 - 103 Actinoids	104 Rf Rutherfordium (267)	105 Db Dubnium (268)	106 Sg Seaborgium (269)	107 Bh Bohrium (270)	108 Hs Hassium (269)	109 Mt Meitnerium (278)	110 Ds Darmstadtium (281)

57 La Lanthanum 138.90547	58 Ce Cerium 140.116	59 Pr Praseodymium 140.90766	60 Nd Neodymium 144.242	61 Pm Promethium (145)	62 Sm Samarium 150.36	63 Eu Europium 151.964	64 Gd Gadolinium 157.25
89 Ac Actinium (227)	90 Th Thorium 232.0377	91 Pa Protactinium 231.03588	92 U Uranium 238.02891	93 Np Neptunium (237)	94 Pu Plutonium (244)	95 Am Americium (243)	96 Cm Curium (247)

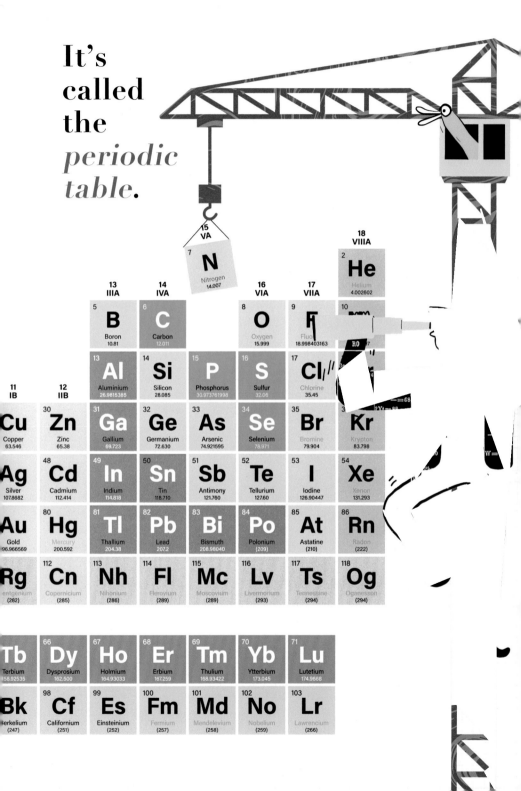

The periodic table lists all 118 elements in order of the number of particles that make up their atoms. That number is called the *atomic number*.

ATOMIC NUMBER

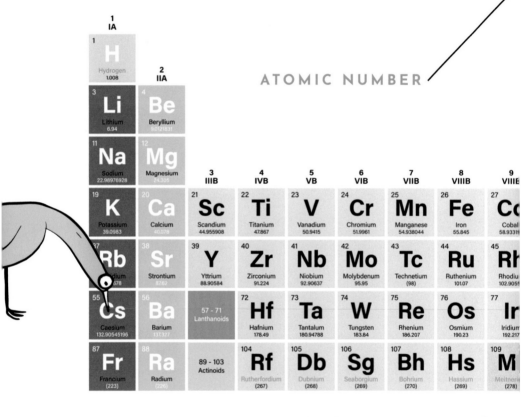

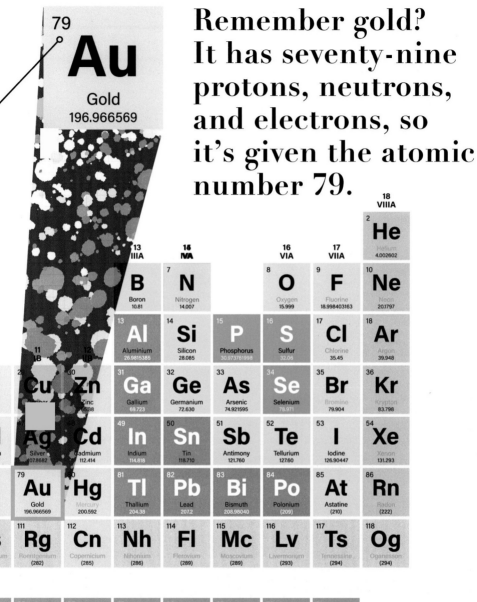

79

Au

Gold
196.966569

Remember gold?
It has seventy-nine
protons, neutrons,
and electrons, so
it's given the atomic
number 79.

The number at the bottom tells us the mass of each atom.

The different colors group elements into families of similar characteristics.

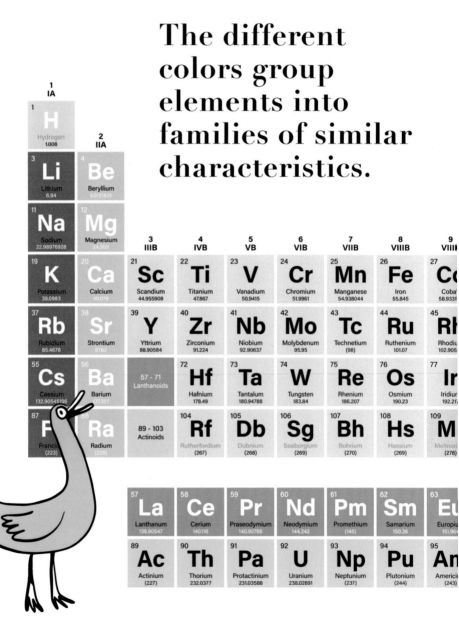

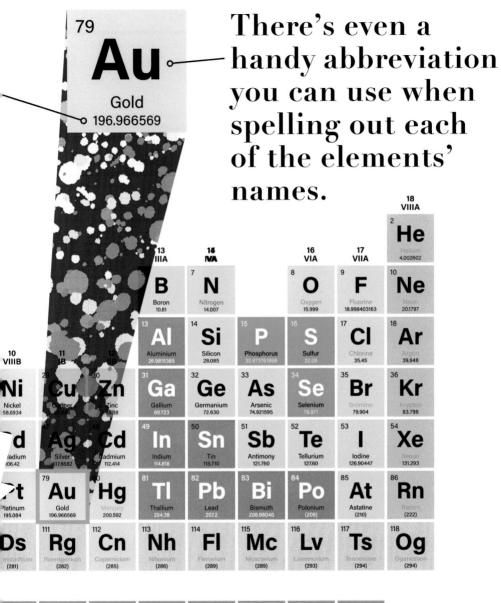

There's even a handy abbreviation you can use when spelling out each of the elements' names.

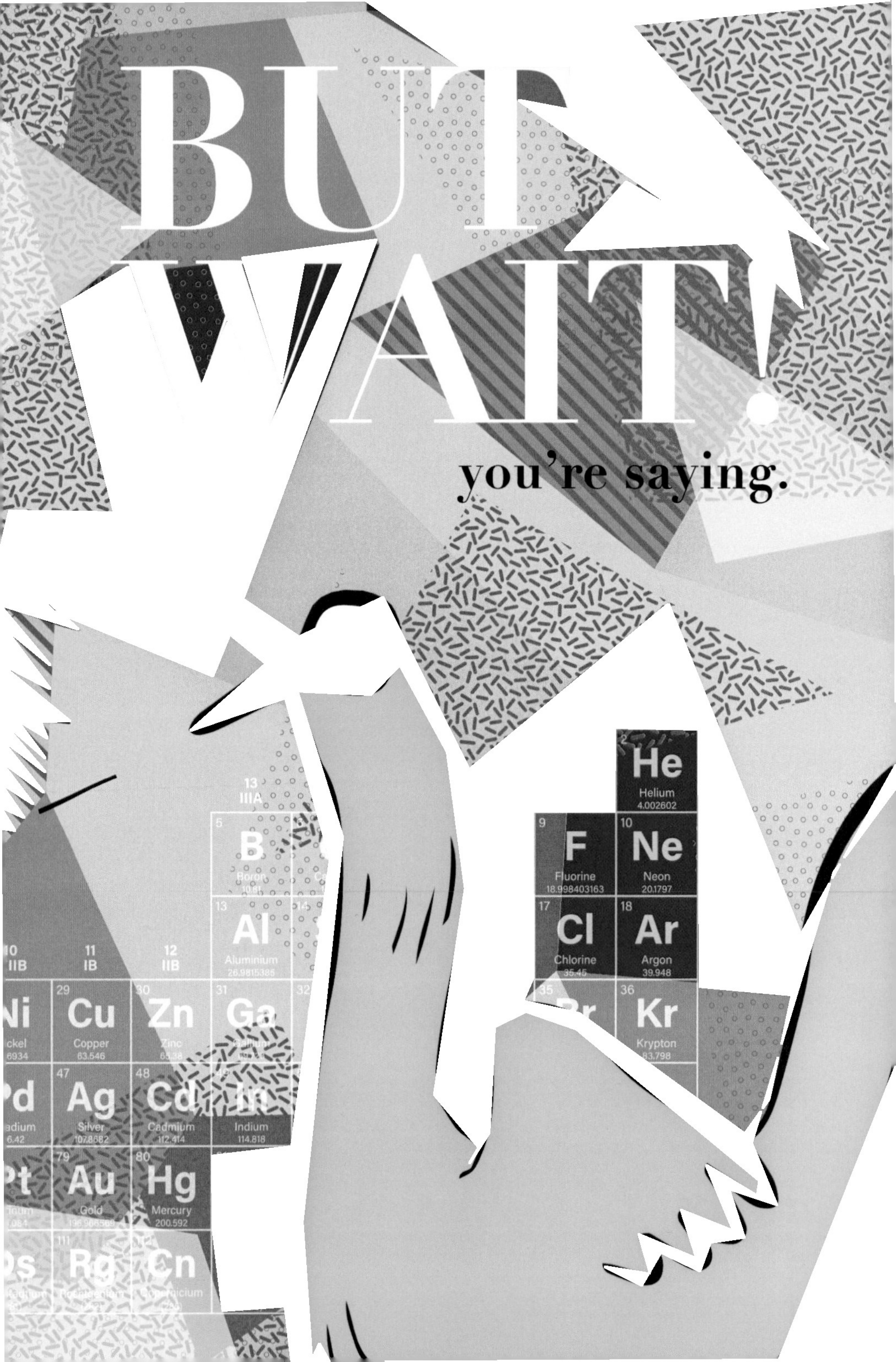
BUT WAIT!
you're saying.
13 IIIA
5 B Boron
13 Al Aluminium 26.9815385
11 IB
12 IIB
29 Cu Copper 63.546
30 Zn Zinc 65.38
31 Ga
47 Ag Silver 107.8682
48 Cd Cadmium 112.414
49 In Indium 114.818
79 Au Gold
80 Hg Mercury 200.592
2 He Helium 4.002602
9 F Fluorine 18.998403163
10 Ne Neon 20.1797
17 Cl Chlorine 35.45
18 Ar Argon 39.948
36 Kr Krypton 83.798

If everything is made up of elements, how come there isn't an element called "Pizza"?

206

Pi

Pizza

And there's certainly no "Stinky Sockium" on there anywhere.

608

Ss

Stinky Sockium

You're right! That's because most of what you see around you isn't made from just one type of element.

Atoms of different elements like to stick together, and when they do, they build new structures. These are called *molecules*, and they're held together by bonds.

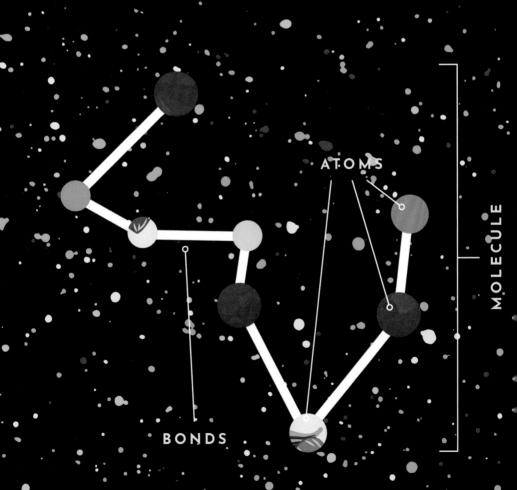

ATOMS

MOLECULE

BONDS

Take a look at hydrogen (that's number 1 on the periodic table) and oxygen (that's number 8). When two hydrogen atoms stick to one oxygen atom, they create a molecule of something you might have seen before . . .

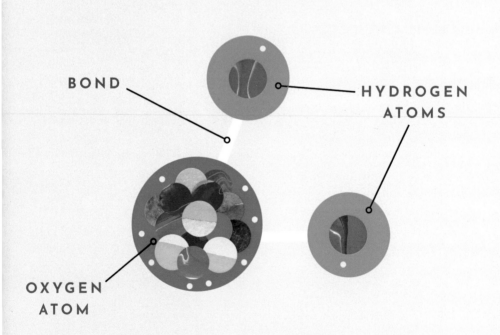

BOND

HYDROGEN ATOMS

OXYGEN ATOM

WATER.

Of course, it takes around

1,500,000,000,000,00

of these molecules to
form a single drop!

OOO

0,000,

0,

That's 1.5 sextillion.

Solid/Liquid/Vapor triple-point

John Dalton was the one who first introduced atomic theory.

Scientists created a convenient way to record what's inside a molecule. They call this a *formula*.

First, they write the abbreviation from the periodic table for each element in the molecule.

Abbreviations were this guy's idea, actually. Meet Jöns Jacob Berzelius.

Then, they write a tiny number to tell how many of that element's atoms are in the molecule. Put it all together, and the formula for water looks like this:

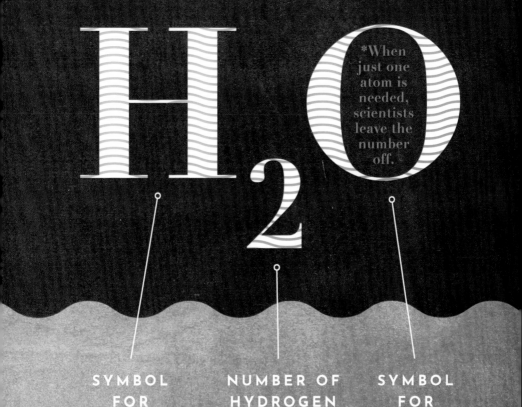

H₂O

*When just one atom is needed, scientists leave the number off.

SYMBOL FOR HYDROGEN

NUMBER OF HYDROGEN ATOMS

SYMBOL FOR OXYGEN*

Here are some formulas for other common substances.

$$C_{12}H_{22}O_{11}$$

TABLE SUGAR
(ALSO CALLED
***SUCROSE*)**

$$CaCO_3$$

CHALK
(ALSO CALLED
CALCIUM
CARBONATE)

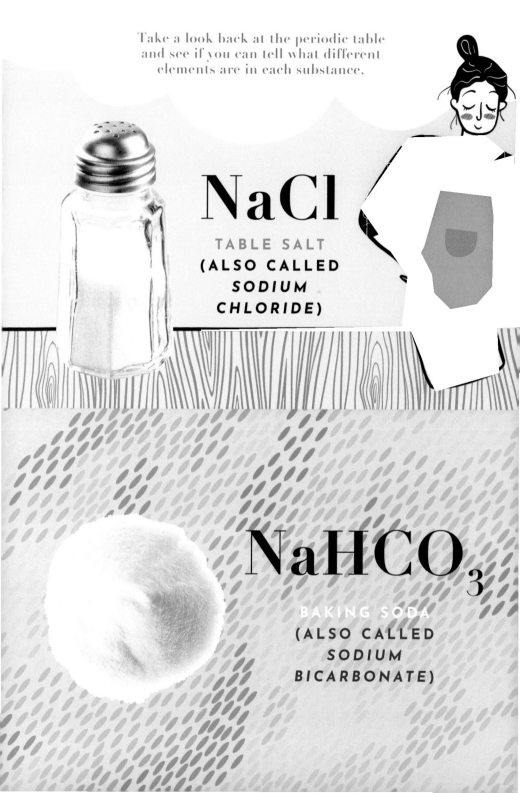

Take a look back at the periodic table and see if you can tell what different elements are in each substance.

NaCl

TABLE SALT
(ALSO CALLED *SODIUM CHLORIDE*)

NaHCO$_3$

BAKING SODA
(ALSO CALLED *SODIUM BICARBONATE*)

More complex items are made of *many* different molecules. Just look at what it takes to make a chocolate chip cookie!*

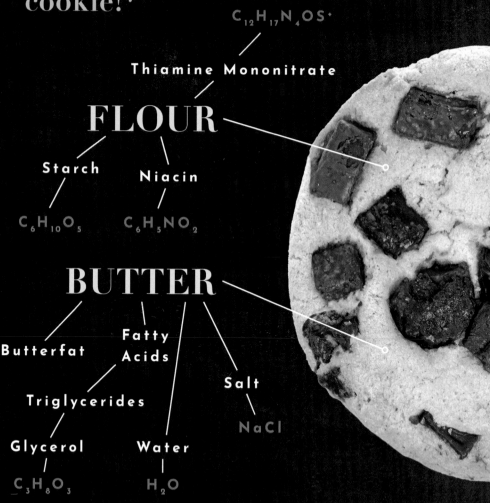

$C_{12}H_{17}N_4OS^+$

Thiamine Mononitrate

FLOUR

Starch

Niacin

$C_6H_{10}O_5$

$C_6H_5NO_2$

BUTTER

Butterfat

Fatty Acids

Triglycerides

Salt

Glycerol

Water

NaCl

$C_3H_8O_3$

H_2O

*This is actually *VERY* simplified. In chocolate alone, there are more than eight hundred different molecules!

$C_3H_7NO_3$

Glutamic Acid — $C_5H_9NO_4$

Serine

Leucine — $C_6H_{13}NO_2$

EGGS — Lysine — $C_6H_{14}N_2O_2$

Water

SUGAR — $C_{12}H_{22}O_{11}$

H_2O

NaCl

SALT

$NaHCO_3$

BAKING SODA

$C_{35}H_{66}NO_7P$

Soy Lecithin

CHOCOLATE CHIPS

Milk Fat

Sugar

Glycerides

$C_{12}H_{22}O_{11}$

Butyric Acid

Cocoa Butter

Cocoa Bean

Palmitic Acid

Oleic Acid

Stearic Acid

$C_4H_8O_2$

Theobromine

$C_7H_8N_4O_2$

$C_{16}H_{32}O_2$

$C_{18}H_{34}O_2$

$C_{18}H_{36}O_2$

And that's
nothing compared
to *living* things.

Like Friedrich Wöhler,
the father of organic
chemistry. Though
technically, he's dead.

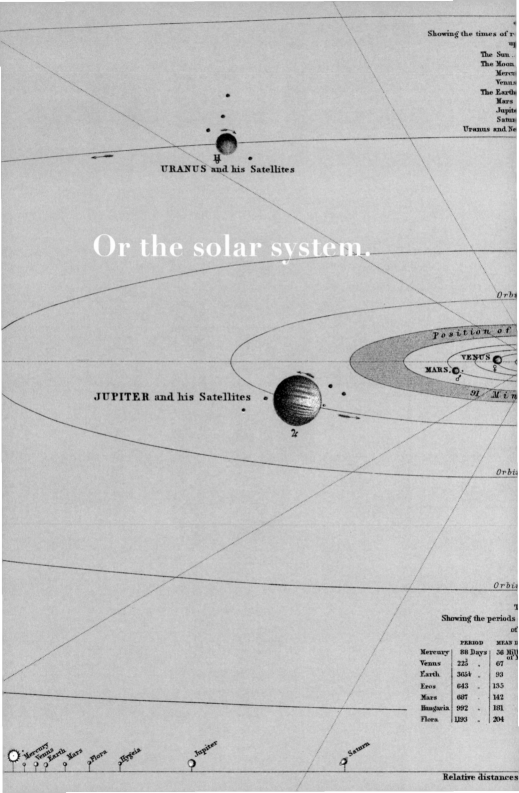

Or the solar system.

URANUS and his Satellites

JUPITER and his Satellites

VENUS

MARS.

Orbi

Position of

91 Min

Orbi

Orbi

Showing the periods
of

	PERIOD	MEAN D
Mercury	88 Days	36 Mill
Venus	225 "	67
Earth	365¼ "	93
Eros	643 "	155
Mars	687 "	142
Hungaria	992 "	181
Flora	1193 "	204

Mercury Venus Earth Mars Flora Hygeia Jupiter Saturn

Relative distances

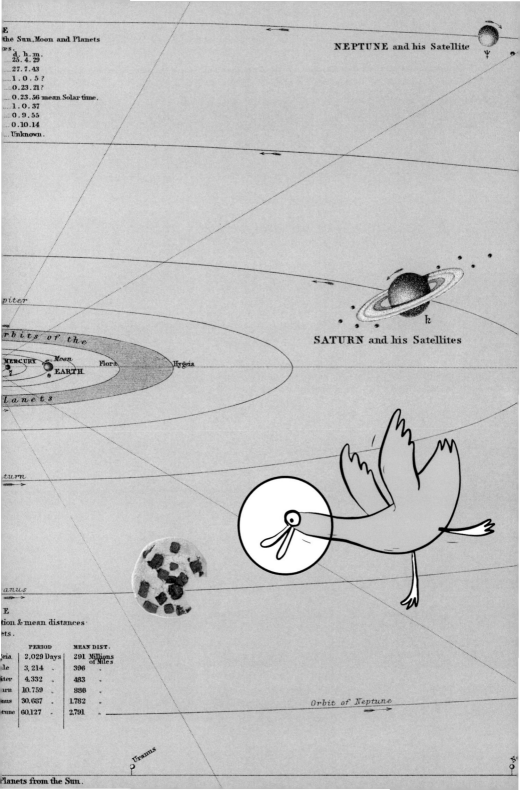

E
the Sun, Moon and Planets
æs.
    d. h. m.
  25. 4. 29
  27. 7. 43
  1 . 0 . 5 ?
  0 . 23 . 21 ?
  0 . 23 . 56 mean Solar time .
  1 . 0 . 37
  0 . 9 . 55
  0 . 10 . 14
  Unknown .

NEPTUNE and his Satellite ♆ ♆

piter

SATURN and his Satellites ♄

rbits of the

MERCURY Moon Flora   Hygeia
EARTH

lanets

turn

anus

E
tion & mean distances
ets .

	PERIOD	MEAN DIST.
geia	2,029 Days	291 Millions of Miles
le	3,214 „	396 „
iter	4,332 „	483 „
arn	10,759 „	838 „
nus	30,687 „	1,782 „
tune	60,127 „	2,791 „

Orbit of Neptune

Uranus ♅

Planets from the Sun .

Or the
entire
bloomin'
universe.

So, you see that atom over there?

Give him a high five.

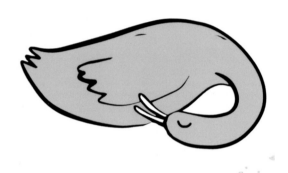

You have a *lot* to thank him for.

GLOSSARY

atom: the smallest piece of an element that still has its unique characteristics

molecule: a unique formation of atoms bonded together that forms the smallest piece of a substance

proton: a positively charged particle found in an atom's nucleus

neutron: a particle with no charge found in nearly every atom's nucleus

electron: a negatively charged particle found outside an atom's nucleus

nucleus: the center core of an atom, made from equal numbers of protons and neutrons and responsible for nearly all the mass of the atom

planetary model: a theoretical model of the atom proposed by Niels Bohr in 1915, in which electrons orbit the nucleus

quantum mechanical model: a theoretical model of the atom proposed by Erwin Schrödinger, in which electrons are positioned outside the nucleus and act like waves

element: a substance with identical properties throughout and made up entirely of one kind of atom

periodic table: a chart that organizes the elements and their characteristics

atomic number: an element's assigned number on the periodic chart, representing the number of protons in the atom

atomic mass: the mass of one atom

bond: the force that holds two atoms together

formula: an abbreviated way of writing the composition and number of atoms in a molecule

atomic expert: you, after reading this book

"The important thing is not to stop questioning. Curiosity has its own reason for existence."

—ALBERT EINSTEIN
1879-1955

A BRIEF HISTORY OF ATOMIC RESEARCH

5th Century BC

Democritus, a Greek philosopher, first proposes the idea of atoms, though his theory is largely ignored for hundreds of years.

1913

Neils Bohr takes Rutherford's theory one step further by proposing that electrons exist in various orbits around the nucleus, each with different energy levels.

1911

Ernest Rutherford, Thomson's former student, disproves the "plum pudding model" when his gold foil experiment uncovers that electrons must be on the outside of a central nucleus.

1926

Erwin Schrödinger introduces the quantum mechanical model when he proposes that electrons instead function like waves of energy.

1932

James Chadwick discovers that atoms also have neutrons.

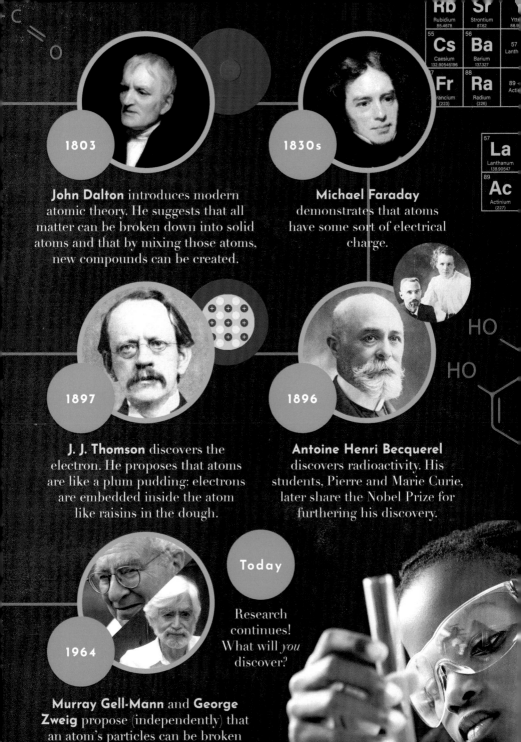

1803

John Dalton introduces modern atomic theory. He suggests that all matter can be broken down into solid atoms and that by mixing those atoms, new compounds can be created.

1830s

Michael Faraday demonstrates that atoms have some sort of electrical charge.

1897

J. J. Thomson discovers the electron. He proposes that atoms are like a plum pudding: electrons are embedded inside the atom like raisins in the dough.

1896

Antoine Henri Becquerel discovers radioactivity. His students, Pierre and Marie Curie, later share the Nobel Prize for furthering his discovery.

1964

Today

Research continues! What will *you* discover?

Murray Gell-Mann and **George Zweig** propose (independently) that an atom's particles can be broken down further into quarks.

SOURCES CONSULTED

American Egg Board. *Egg Products Reference Guide*. Park Ridge, IL: American Egg Board, 2006. https://www.aeb.org/images/website/documents/food-manufacturers/order-aeb-resources/Egg_Products_Reference_Guide.pdf.

Helmenstine, Anne Marie. "How Many Molecules Are in a Drop of Water?" ThoughtCo. https://www.thoughtco.com/atoms-in-a-drop-of-water-609425.

Barad, Karen Michelle. Essay. In *Meeting the Universe Halfway: Quantum Physics and the Entanglement of Matter and Meaning*, 254. Durham: Duke University Press, 2007.

Bergmann, Jon. "Transcript of 'Just How Small Is an Atom?'." TED. https://www.ted.com/talks/jon_bergmann_just_how_small_is_an_atom/transcript?language=en.

Blackman, Eric G. "The Bohr Model." Department of Physics and Astronomy. University of Rochester. https://www.pas.rochester.edu/~blackman/ast104/bohr.html.

"Butter." Wikipedia. Wikimedia Foundation, April 8, 2021. https://en.wikipedia.org/wiki/Butter.

"Chemicals - Formulas and Trading Names." Engineering ToolBox. https://www.engineeringtoolbox.com/chemicals-formulas-trade-names-d_1758.html.

"The Chemistry of Chocolate – Biomedical Beat Blog." National Institute of General Medical Sciences. U.S. Department of Health and Human Services. https://biobeat.nigms.nih.gov/2020/02/the-chemistry-of-chocolate/.

"Death of a Genius." *Life*, May 2, 1955.

"Development of the Atomic Theory." http://www.abcte.org/files/previews/chemistry/s1_p6.html.

"Does an Electron in an Atom Move at All?" Science Questions with Surprising Answers. https://wtamu.edu/~cbaird/sq/2014/12/01/does-an-electron-in-an-atom-move-at-all.

"Glutamic Acid." Wikipedia. Wikimedia Foundation, April 13, 2021. https://en.wikipedia.org/wiki/Glutamic_acid.

"Important Chemical Compounds- Their Common Names, Formula and Uses." PendulumEdu. https://pendulumedu.com/general-awareness/list-of-chemical-compounds-formula-uses-and-their-common-name.

Kurzgesagt - In a Nutshell. *How Small Is An Atom? Spoiler: Very Small*. YouTube. YouTube, 2015. https://www.youtube.com/watch?v=_lNF3_3olUE.

"Lecithin from Soybean." National Center for Biotechnology Information. PubChem Compound Database. U.S. National Library of Medicine. Accessed April 29, 2021. https://pubchem.ncbi.nlm.nih.gov/compound/Lecithin-from-Soybean.

"Leucine." Wikipedia. Wikimedia Foundation, April 11, 2021. https://en.wikipedia.org/wiki/Leucine.

"Lysine." Wikipedia. Wikimedia Foundation, March 19, 2021. https://en.wikipedia.org/wiki/Lysine.

"Nicotinic Acid." National Center for Biotechnology Information. PubChem Compound Database. U.S. National Library of Medicine. https://pubchem.ncbi.nlm.nih.gov/compound/Nicotinic-acid.

No. 2627: The Bohr-Einstein Debates. https://www.uh.edu/engines/epi2627.htm.

O'Luanaigh, Cian. "Fifty Years of Quarks." CERN. https://home.cern/news/news/physics/fifty-years-quarks.

"Propulsion." What is an ion? Accessed April 29, 2021. https://www.qrg.northwestern.edu/projects/vss/docs/Propulsion/1-what-is-an-ion.html.

"The Quantum Mechanical Model of the Atom (Article)." Khan Academy. Khan Academy. https://www.khanacademy.org/science/physics/quantum-physics/quantum-numbers-and-orbitals/a/the-quantum-mechanical-model-of-the-atom.

"Serine." Wikipedia. Wikimedia Foundation, March 5, 2021. https://en.wikipedia.org/wiki/Serine.

"Sodium Chloride." Wikipedia. Wikimedia Foundation, April 22, 2021. https://en.wikipedia.org/wiki/Sodium_chloride.

"Sugar." *Encyclopædia Britannica*. Encyclopædia Britannica, Inc. https://www.britannica.com/science/sugar-chemical-compound.

"Thiamine." Wikipedia. Wikimedia Foundation, March 31, 2021. https://en.wikipedia.org/wiki/Thiamine.

"What Is the Chemical Formula for Chalk?" Reference. IAC Publishing. https://www.reference.com/science/chemical-formula-chalk-22ad5a46d87231a5.

"What Is the Chemical Formula for Wheat Flour?" Reference. IAC Publishing. https://www.reference.com/science/chemical-formula-wheat-flour-677c04b3c46e01cd.

ABOUT THE AUTHOR

David Miles is an award-winning and bestselling author and illustrator of over forty books, including *Book*, *The Interactive Constitution*, *Allegro*, *Unicorn (and Horse)*, and other titles. He's been named a Cybils Award Finalist, *Publishers Weekly* Star Watch Nominee, TRVST Changemaker, New York Book Show Award Winner, and Bill Fisher Award Finalist, among other accolades. He lives in Fresno, California, with his family.

If you liked this book, please leave a review online at your favorite retailer. Honest reviews spread the word about Bushel & Peck—and help us make better books, too!

For Stephanie, our nucleus.

And for Ronald Lease, an
extraordinary teacher.